W9-BUR-013

PIRATES!

CRACK THE PIRATE CODE

by Liam O'Donnell

capstone

© 2018 Heinemann-Raintree
an imprint of Capstone Global Library, LLC
Chicago, Illinois

To contact Capstone Global Library please call 800-747-4992, or visit our web site
www.mycapstone.com

All rights reserved. No part of this publication may be reproduced or transmitted in any form
or by any means, electronic or mechanical, including photocopying, recording, taping, or any
information storage and retrieval system, without permission in writing from the publisher.

Library of Congress
Cataloging-in-Publication data is available on the Library of Congress website.

ISBN 978-1-4109-8706-8 (library binding)
ISBN 978-1-4109-8710-5 (paperback)
ISBN 978-1-4109-8722-8 (eBook PDF)

Summary:
Avast! The oceans are filled with pirates! But pirates have a code to follow. Read this book to learn about the
code that guided pirates' lives.

Editorial Credits
Bradley Cole, editor; Kayla Dohmen, designer; Wanda Winch, media researcher,
Katy LaVigne, production specialist

Photo Credits
We would like to thank the following for permission to reproduce photographs: Alamy Stock Photo: Lebrecht
Music and Arts Photo Library, 25; Bridgeman Images: © Look and Learn/Private Collection/Kenneth John
Petts, 7, © Look and Learn/Private Collection/Ron Embleton, 13, 21, 23, 29, Peter Newark Historical Pictures/
Private Collection/Arthur David McCormick, 9; Capstone: Roger Stewart, 19; Getty Images Inc: Bettmann,
17; iStockphoto: JohnGollop, cover (map top, bottom); Paul Daly, 27; Rick Reeves: rickreevesstudio.com, 5,
11; Shutterstock: Andrey Armyagov, cover (middle), Andrey_Kuzmin, 2-3 background, Antony McAulay, 26,
grafvision, cover (right), ilolab, vintage paper texture, Melkor3D, 15, Molodec, maps, Nik Merkulov, grunge
background, pingebat, pirate icons, sharpner, map directions to island treasure, Triff, nautical background,
TyBy, cover (banner)

Printed and bound in China.
004627

TABLE OF CONTENTS

Some words are shown in bold, **like this**. You can find out what they mean by looking in the glossary.

Equal Treatment

Pirate ships were crowded and dirty. Pirates were nearly always tired, wet, and cold. Why did pirates choose to live like this? Because the Pirate **Code** said that they would all be treated the same. It also promised an equal share in any treasure!

Fact

Ships often had many beetles and rats. These pests carried **diseases** that spread quickly. Sometimes half of a ship's **crew** could die from disease.

Working Together

Pirates made their living by stealing. They looked for ships carrying gold, spices, weapons, and other gear that they could steal.

But pirates had to work hard to get the treasure. The Pirate Code made sure that everyone did his job.

Fact

Even people could be treasure. Pirates sometimes **kidnapped** ship doctors and **carpenters**. They also kidnapped and sold some people as **slaves**.

Rules

Every pirate ship had its own list of rules. Before any man joined, he had to first sign the ship's code. He had to swear his **loyalty** over the Bible or an axe. The pirate could then take a share of any stolen treasure.

Fact

Pirate captains asked men if they had wives or families. If they did, they usually weren't allowed to join the crew.

Pirates could usually **vote** on where they sailed and what ships to attack. If the crew didn't like a captain's idea, they wouldn't do it. Pirate crews also voted on who would be their captain. They could just as easily vote him out!

Fact

While on a job for the British government in 1692, Captain Thomas Tew suggested searching for treasure instead. His crew agreed and they became pirates.

Women Pirates

On many ships, the code said women were not allowed on board. Many pirates thought women were bad luck.

But some women actually became pirates. Anne Bonny and Mary Read sailed with "Calico Jack" Rackham during the early 1700s. They usually dressed as men.

Fact

When their ship was captured in 1720, Bonny and Read continued to fight when all the men hid below **deck**.

Lights Out!

Piracy was hard work, and pirates needed their sleep. Many ship rules stated that all candles and lamps had to be put out by 8 p.m. This helped to prevent fires and avoided giving away the ship's location to the pirates' enemies.

Fact

If any pirates wished to stay up past 8 p.m., they would have to sit on the deck in the dark.

Ready to Fight

The Pirate Code said that every pirate had to keep his weapons clean. The weapons had to be ready to use. If a pirate let his sword get rusty or his pistol become dirty, he would face **punishment**.

Fact

If a pirate ran away from battle or refused to fight, he would be punished when the fight was over.

Dividing the Treasure

According to the code, each pirate received a share of treasure based on his job. The more important a pirate's job, the bigger his share of the treasure. The captain usually got two shares. Most crewmembers got only one share.

Fact

The code on many ships promised extra money to pirates who lost arms or legs in battle.

Breaking the Code

Pirates were feared for their cruel crimes. But pirates often suffered cruel punishment as well. Pirates who broke the Pirate Code could be marooned. A marooned person was left behind on a deserted island, far from any other people. He was given little food or water.

Fact

Pirates who killed a crewmate were forced to do the "Murderer's Swim." First, the pirate was tied to the dead body. Then he was thrown overboard and left to drown.

Pirates were punished if they were caught stealing from each other. One punishment was to cut off the thief's nose or ears. Then he was left ashore. Authorities would have likely recognized him as a pirate and punished him for his crimes.

Fact
Walking the plank is the most famous pirate punishment. However, it's unlikely that it ever really happened!

Another way to punish a thief was to tie him to the **main** of the ship. The pirate was left without food or water for days. He was often beaten. Sometimes the other pirates circled around him. They jabbed at him with their daggers and swords.

Fact
Pirates would sometimes rub salt or vinegar into the thief's open wounds.

Flogging

Flogging kept pirates from fighting each other or breaking other rules. This punishment was done with a special whip called the cat-o'-nine-tails. It had nine ropes attached to a handle. Each rope had knots tied into it. Flogging often caused large, painful cuts.

Fact
Sometimes fishhooks or other sharp objects were tied to the ends of a cat-o'-nine-tails.

Code for Success

Some of the punishments for breaking the Pirate Code were very cruel. But the code made sure pirates lived and worked well together. Without rules, pirates wouldn't have been very successful.

Fact

Sailors were sometimes punished by keelhauling. This involved the sailor being tied with a rope and pulled under the ship. His body was cut by razor-sharp **barnacles**. Most victims drowned.

GLOSSARY

barnacles small shellfish that are covered in very hard shells; barnacles attach themselves to the sides of ships

carpenter someone who works with wood

code collection of rules that a group of people have to live by

crew group of people who work on a ship

deck upper floor of a ship

deserted empty or abandoned

disease sickness or illness

flogging beating someone with a whip or stick

kidnap capture someone and hold them until you get what you want

location the exact place where someone or something is

loyalty strong feeling of support for other people

mainmast tall post in the center of a ship to which the main sails are attached

punishment action that is carried out against someone to stop them doing something

slave person who is owned by another person. Slaves were forced to work for no money.

vote choice made by a person based on their own views

READ MORE

Books

Lock, Deborah. *Pirates*. Eyewonder. New York, NY: DK Publishing, 2015.

Platt, Richard. *Pirate Diary*. Diary Histories. Cambridge, MA: Candlewick Press, 2014.

Vonne, Mira. *Gross Facts About Pirates*. Gross History. North Mankato, MN: Capstone Press, 2017.

Internet Sites

Use FactHound to find Internet sites related to this book.:

Visit *www.facthound.com*

Just type in 9781410987068 and go.

 Check out projects, games and lots more at
www.capstonekids.com

INDEX

battle 16, 19
beetles 4
Bonny, Anne 12, 13

candles 14
captains 8, 10, 18
carpenters 6
cat-o'-nine-tails 26, 27

diseases 4
doctors 6

families 8
flogging 26

jobs 6, 10, 18
joining 8

keelhauling 28
kidnapping 6

lamps 14
loyalty 8

marooning 20
Murderer's Swim 20

pistols 16
punishments 16, 20, 22, 24,
 25, 26, 28

Rackham, "Calico" Jack 12
rats 4
Read, Mary 12, 13

sharing 4, 8, 18, 19
ships 4, 6, 8, 10, 12, 13, 14, 19,
 24, 28
slavery 6
sleep 14
stealing 6, 22, 24
swords 16, 24

Tew, Thomas 10
treasure 4, 6, 8, 10, 18

voting 10

walking the plank 22
weapons 6, 16, 24
women 12